viewpoint

CONTENTS

SEAL CULL   2

WHALING   12

ANIMAL TESTING   18

written by Ryan Hutchings

illustrated by Serena Kearns

Captain Nichola
Goddard School

Seal Cull

THE HERALD | NEWS |

SEARCH

HOME News Sport World Weather Property Lifestyle Business Jobs Subscribe Readers' Forum

THOUSANDS OF SEALS DIE ON THE ICE IN CANADA'S ANNUAL HUNT

Hundreds of seal hunters arrived on the ice of Newfoundland yesterday at the start of Canada's annual seal cull — the world's largest marine mammal hunt. Over the next few weeks, hundreds of thousands of harp seal pups will be clubbed to death and skinned, their fur sold to meet demand from the European fashion market.

Canada's annual seal cull has been the cause of protest and controversy for decades. The hunt starts when the pups are only two weeks old, when their fur changes from white to grey. There are strict guidelines surrounding the killing of the pups and hunters claim that the methods they use have made the killing as humane as possible. **THEY ARE REQUIRED TO PERFORM A BLINKING REFLEX TEST BY TOUCHING THE EYE OF THE SEAL TO CHECK THAT IT IS DEAD BEFORE SKINNING.**

HUNTED — THE HARP SEAL PUP

However, animal rights activists, who have a strong presence at the cull, claim the pups are often skinned alive as the hunters work hastily to take as many skins as they can. According to one activist present at the cull, tests have shown that as many as 42 per cent of clubbed seals were still conscious when their skins were taken.

1 2

supposition: *According to one activist present at the cull, tests have shown that as many as 42 per cent of clubbed seals were still conscious when their skins were taken.* **Is this supposition? Why/why not?**

✱ SUPPOSITION: AN IDEA OR OPINION THAT IS FORMED ON THE BASIS OF LIMITED EVIDENCE, RATHER THAN REAL PROOF.

THE HERALD | NEWS | SEARCH ⟳

HOME News Sport World Weather Property Lifestyle Business Jobs Subscribe Readers' Forum

Opposition to the annual seal hunt in the 1980s led to a decline in the seal fur trade and the European Union banned import of fur from pups younger than three weeks old. However, a decline in the cod populations off the Newfoundland coast since the 1990s has led to a call for increased seal hunting quotas. The issue gained attention again in 2003 when the Canadian Government set a quota to cull a million seals over three years.

The government claims the annual seal hunt contributes a significant amount to the economy and is a **VITAL SOURCE OF EMPLOYMENT** FOR LOCAL FISHERMEN.

This year's quota will now see more than a quarter of a million of the estimated 5.2 million seal population killed. Although harp seals are not endangered, some scientists predict that if the annual hunt quota remains this high, the harp seal population could be reduced by 70 per cent in the next 15 years.

Animal activists hope that fur will fall out of fashion as consumers become more ecologically conscious, putting an end to a tradition seen by many as barbaric.

READERS' FORUM: POST YOUR COMMENTS

PROUDHUNTA | POSTED: 8.31AM |

I am a seal hunter frustrated with the animal activists giving us a bad reputation through misinformation. For example, your story appears alongside a photograph of a white-coated seal pup. It is illegal to hunt these harp seal pups (as well as the black-coated hooded seal pups) and has been since 1987. These images are used by anti-sealing groups hoping to get an emotional response.

We need to put people before animals. Sealing is a valuable source of employment for some of the communities on the eastern seaboard of Canada, a relatively poor part of the country. In Newfoundland and Labrador, the annual seal hunt contributes $55 million to the local economy. **THESE COMMUNITIES COULDN'T SURVIVE WITHOUT THAT REVENUE.**

inference:

[
We need to put people before animals.
]

WHAT CAN YOU INFER ABOUT WHAT THE WRITER IS IMPLYING HERE? IS THIS AN ATTEMPT TO MANIPULATE PUBLIC OPINION ABOUT ANIMAL ACTIVISTS? **WHY/WHY NOT?**

beyond the text:

HOW CAN THE PROVISION OF JOBS FOR PEOPLE IN THE SEAL CULLING INDUSTRY AND THE PROTECTION OF SEAL PUPS BE BETTER BALANCED?

NEWFOUNDLAND

NORTHERN OCEAN

THE ATLANTIC COD

Many people in this area used to be employed in the fishing industry, but the severe depletion of Atlantic cod numbers has meant a number of people have lost their jobs. The unemployment rate in this area is now around 14 per cent. Not only does the seal hunt provide valuable employment opportunities through hunting, it will also help the fishing industry with the regeneration of Atlantic cod numbers.

At present there are around 5.8 million seals in the area, three times the herd number in the 1970s. The seal cull is necessary to keep numbers down to a sustainable level. Some people may find the thought unpleasant, but the cull is necessary.

research:

At present there are around 5.8 million seals in the area, three times the herd number in the 1970s.

HOW COULD YOU VALIDATE THESE STATISTICS?

WE NEED TO PUT PEOPLE BEFORE ANIMALS...

READERS' FORUM: POST YOUR COMMENTS

 ANIMALUVA | POSTED: 9.22AM |

The seal cull is inhumane, unnecessary and unprofitable.

The Canadian Government wants us to believe that the seal population is out of control. It is true that numbers have increased from the 1970s. However, the harp seal population is less than a quarter of what it was before Europeans arrived on the continent. If seal numbers really are too high then surely this will be balanced by nature.

Your article refers to the annual seal hunt contributing a significant amount to the economy. The seal cull earns Canada $16 million in meat and pelt sales. Yet around the same amount of money is spent in policing and administrating the cull. In Newfoundland, where 90 per cent of the sealers live, the cull contributes only one per cent of the region's GDP (Gross Domestic Product).

persuasive language:

HAS THE WRITER ANIMALUVA USED EMOTIVE LANGUAGE TO MANIPULATE YOUR FEELINGS? **WHY/WHY NOT?**

WHAT IMPACT DOES THE IMAGE OF THE SEAL PUP HAVE ON YOU?

visual features:

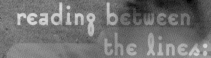

reading between the lines:

There are too many humans on this planet, not seals. **WHAT DOES THIS STATEMENT SUGGEST ABOUT THE WRITER?**

POST YOUR COMMENTS

The article also talks about the cull being a "vital source of employment for local fishermen". However, in Newfoundland, around half a million people are employed in the fishing industry. Of these, only 4000 take part in the seal cull.

The Canadian Government is using the harp seal as a scapegoat for their own over-fishing in the region. THERE ARE TOO MANY HUMANS ON THIS PLANET, **NOT SEALS.** SHAME ON YOU, CANADA!

SHAME ON **YOU**, CANADA!

SAVE THE SEALS

SAVE

Save the

READERS' FORUM: POST YOUR COMMENTS

FUR4EVA | POSTED: 10.01AM |

I am a supporter of the seal cull for ethical reasons. I consider hunted fur to be not only the environmentally friendly choice but also more humane than the alternatives.

Your article talks about "fur [falling] out of fashion as consumers become more ecologically conscious". Fur is a natural product – it is renewable and biodegradable and offers considerable warmth to the wearer.

The alternative to fur is damaging to the environment. All fake fur is made from synthetic materials, including polyester and nylon. These materials are responsible for the pollution of waterways from large-scale factory production. Nylon production also creates as much as 50 per cent of the poisonous greenhouse gas nitrous oxide that is polluting the environment.

Polyester is petroleum-based. Petroleum is a non-renewable, precious natural resource that will one day run out. We need to start limiting its unnecessary use.

...FUR HUNTING IS ALSO MORE HUMANE

Fur hunting is also more humane. Each year, the number of seals culled is lower than the number of animals killed annually in European fur farms, where the animals are farmed intensively and have a poor quality of life. At least the Canadian seals live happily in their natural environment before they are killed.

A lot of anti-seal-cull protesters talk about seals being skinned alive. However, a 2002 report by the *Canadian Veterinary Journal* found that 98 per cent of the seals it examined had been killed humanely. The Federal Department of Fisheries and Oceans has also warned that looks can be deceiving — seals have a swimming reflex that is active even after death. This is similar to the reflex seen in chickens.

It gives the impression of the animal being alive and conscious, even though it is dead.

Hunted fur has been used by people for centuries. It is a natural, eco-friendly product obtained from animals that have lived happily in their environment. **I DON'T PLAN TO STOP** WEARING IT ANYTIME SOON.

analyse:

Fur hunting is also more humane. Each year, the number of seals culled is lower than the number of animals killed annually in European fur farms, where the animals are farmed intensively and have a poor quality of life. **IS THIS A RATIONAL ARGUMENT FOR FUR HUNTING BEING MORE HUMANE?** WHAT DO YOU THINK?

READERS' FORUM: POST YOUR COMMEN

SaveTheSeals | POSTED: 10.44AM |

I was present at the seal cull yesterday as a protester. I was horrified with the scene I witnessed, which was like something out of a horror movie. The ice was stained red with the blood of the slaughtered seals and, when one suffering baby looked straight into my eyes as it lay skinned and dying, I could not help but cry at the brutality.

Your article states that there are "strict guidelines" to make the killing as humane as possible. A number of seals are killed by the hakapik, a primitive device that is like a heavy wooden club, with a hammer head and sharp pick attached. **A 2001 REPORT BY FIVE INDEPENDENT VETERINARIANS FOUND THAT IMPROPER USE OF THE HAKAPIK RESULTED IN "CONSIDERABLE AND UNACCEPTABLE SUFFERING" IN THE ANIMAL.** In fact, in 17 per cent of cases the animal didn't even get struck in the head, meaning that their death was almost certainly slow and painful and that the animal was conscious while being skinned.

emotional appeal:
WHAT FEELINGS ARE EVOKED BY THE WRITER'S DESCRIPTION OF THE SEAL CULL?

READERS' COMMENTS

Only a few decades ago, Canada was a whaling nation. There were people who argued that banning whaling would be severely detrimental to the economy. Yet the economy adjusted and now people travel from all over the world to see the whales off Canada's coastline. The value of tourism in places such as Newfoundland, which at the moment is valued at around $500 million annually, is significantly more than the seal cull. The international community is disgusted by the cull and, if it continues, Canada will not only have to face boycotts of exports, but boycotts on tourism as well.

Ban the seal cull!

persuasive language:

HOW HAS THE AUTHOR USED THE POWER OF WORDS TO MANIPULATE YOUR FEELINGS? **WHAT WORDS HAVE POSITIVE OR NEGATIVE ASSOCIATIONS FOR YOU? WHY?**

summarise:

ARGUMENTS:
- FOR THE SEAL CULL
- AGAINST THE SEAL CULL

HOW WOULD YOU SUMMARISE THE MAIN IDEAS FOR EACH ARGUMENT?

Whaling

Norwegian Whaling Season

RYAN HUTCHINGS REPORTS

OPENS

Despite protests from the international community and environmental groups, Norwegian whaling ships have entered the North Atlantic to begin the annual hunt for minke whales. The whaling season will continue until late August, during which time up to 1052 whales will be slaughtered.

Whales have been hunted for their meat and by-products for more than 8000 years, originally using traditional hunting methods. In the 17th century, whaling developed into a commercial industry with fleets of large whaling ships that could travel to more distant hunting grounds.

For decades whaling has been a topic of much emotive debate. Conservationists concerned about dwindling whale numbers and the suffering of the animals during slaughter have come up against large whaling industries reluctant to give up the practice. Five of the 13 great whales are now listed as endangered.

In 1946, the International Whaling Commission (IWC) was set up, originally for the purpose of developing the whaling industry. However, over time the commission's role has changed and its focus is now on the conservation of whale numbers.

analyse:

DOES THE WRITER PRESENT A BALANCE OF VIEWPOINTS ABOUT THE PROS AND CONS OF WHALING? WHY/WHY NOT?

...UP TO 1052 WHALES WILL BE SLAUGHTERED

In 1986, the IWC introduced a moratorium, or temporary ban, on whaling for its members to help increase whale numbers. However, the Norwegian Government has registered an official objection to the ban. After five years of taking whales only for scientific purposes, Norway resumed commercial whaling in 1993. Since then a quota system has been in place. In 2006 this quota was raised to a total of 1052 whales per year. Prior to the moratorium, Norway caught around 2000 whales per year.

Norway's modern whaling ships use slaughter methods, such as the penthrite grenade harpoon, that they argue are the most humane methods available.

There is only a handful of other nations in the world that also continue to hunt whales. Many native groups in places such as Alaska, Canada and parts of the Caribbean have permission from the IWC to hunt small numbers of whales for local use. Some nations such as Japan skirt the IWC moratorium and claim that whales are caught only for scientific research. These claims have been hotly debated by conservation groups.

In Norway, political pressure as well as the livelihoods of many poor fishermen mean that the commercial hunting of minke whales is unlikely to cease anytime soon.

bias:

Some nations such as Japan skirt the IWC moratorium and claim that whales are caught only for scientific research.

IS AUTHOR BIAS EVIDENT IN THIS STATEMENT? WHY/WHY NOT? HOW DID YOU FORM YOUR OPINION?

To the Director
Whale Protection Organisation
13 August, 2007

Dear Sir/Madam,

I would like to put forward my point of view on the issue of whaling in Norway, an industry that is faced with emotive opposition from organisations such as your own.

In my opinion, this is an argument about personal freedom. It is about our choice as a nation to decide for ourselves about managing our natural resources and the continuation of an important tradition.

Whale meat is a traditional Norwegian meal and is an important part of our culture. Whaling is mentioned in Norwegian literature from as early as the ninth century and hunting minke whales with harpoons has been widespread since the 1200s. My children and I have the right to continue to eat the same food as our forebears.

There is a great deal of misinformation circulated about whaling. Despite what many people believe, modern whaling is sustainable. The whale we hunt is the minke. It is not an endangered species and is managed the same way as any other fishery, such as tuna. The only difference is that the whale happens to be a mammal.

The minke population of the North Atlantic is around 107,000 animals. Our annual quota of around 1000 whales is less than one per cent of this population. The worldwide population of minke is huge.

DRIED WHALE MEAT

analyse:
ANALYSE THE ARGUMENT
SUPPORTING THE CASE FOR
WHALING. HAS IT CHANGED
YOUR THOUGHTS?
WHY/WHY NOT?

POINTS I ACCEPT > REASONS WHY

POINTS I DO NOT ACCEPT > REASONS WHY

...ONE WHALE CAN YIELD UP TO A TONNE OF MEAT

ISSUES:

Is tradition
a valid reason
for continuing
the practice of
whaling? What do
you think?

According to the International Whaling Commission, there are more than 750,000 whales in Antarctic waters alone. That's about the same as the population of San Francisco. Not only are the minke population numbers high, they are also increasing, thanks to sustainable whaling practices.

People who are anti-whaling claim that killing a whale is a waste of a life, yet one whale can yield up to a tonne of meat. That is an extremely efficient use of an animal's life. How many chickens would it take to produce a tonne of meat? Around 750! What's more, virtually every part of the animal is used, including the blubber, so there is very little waste.

Norway is committed to responsible, sustainable whaling. The Norwegian Government has reserved its position on the International Whaling Commission moratorium and we are therefore legally allowed to continue whaling under Article V of the International Convention for the Regulation of Whaling.

I am also tired of hearing people talk about cruelty to whales. This is misinformed. All Norwegian whaling boats use the grenade harpoon and have done so since 1984. This sophisticated piece of equipment means that 80 per cent of the whales die or lose consciousness immediately. Of the remaining 20 per cent, only half survive the first strike and have to be harpooned a second time. This is a humane method and compares favourably with methods employed in livestock slaughterhouses.

What's more, at the beginning of each season, the harpoon gunners must pass a shooting test with both a harpoon and a rifle and they must attend a course on shooting and killing. To ensure that these humane methods are followed, every vessel carries an independent inspector on board to monitor activities. This inspector reports directly to the fishery authorities.

Please take note of my points and reconsider your organisation's stance on whaling. We should be free to pursue this important tradition without pressure and interference from misinformed bullies.

Yours sincerely,

Whale Hunter, Norway

To the Minister for the Environment
Government House
Capital City

Dear Sir/Madam,

I am writing to voice my protest regarding the continuation of whaling by Norwegian vessels. We are now one of the few nations on the planet that continue with this barbaric practice and I urge you to put a ban on commercial whaling immediately.

Pro-whalers cite tradition and culture as an excuse to continue whaling. This is absurd. The human race evolves – we have abolished slavery, we have given women the right to vote, we have adopted sustainable lifestyles, yet these people want us to live in the past and continue to kill and eat beautiful creatures of the sea. What's more, they want to kill more of them than ever before. In 2006 the quota was raised by 30 per cent to 1052 minke whales per year. This will have a serious impact on minke populations for years to come.

Pro-whalers claim that there are huge populations of whales yet, since the resumption of whaling in 1993, the killing quota has rarely been met. In the 2007 season, despite having a quota of 1052 whales, only 592 were killed. It is getting harder and harder for the hunters to find whales. Although it is true that the minke is not endangered, this is not a reason to eat it.

question: HOW DO YOU THINK THE USE OF STATISTICS ENHANCES THIS ARGUMENT? RESEARCH THEIR CREDIBILITY.

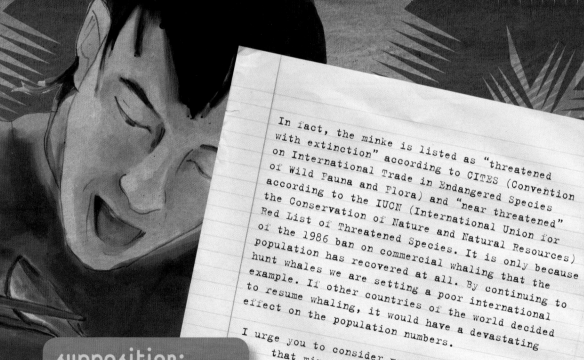

supposition:

I urge you to consider my protest and to realise that mine is not a lone voice. It is the opinion of all of my friends and family and, I believe, every young person in Norway. IS THIS SUPPOSITION? WHY/WHY NOT?

Animal Testing

Anti-Vivisection Protests Expected at Science Research Convention

Organisers of a science convention being held at the university this Friday are concerned that animal rights protestors could disrupt proceedings and attract negative attention to their research.

Vivisection is the practice of testing on live animals in science laboratories. It is estimated that 50 to 100 million animals are tested on worldwide every year. They range from rodents and fish to primates. Much of this testing is undertaken to help find cures for serious human illnesses.

For decades scientists and animal rights activists have clashed over their opposing views on vivisection. Scientists claim that the greater good of helping humankind outweighs the suffering of lab animals. The activists argue that all creatures have the right to life and that testing on animals is cruel and unnecessary.

In 1984, the World Health Organization's Council for International Organizations of Medical Sciences (CIOMS) released the International Guiding Principles for Biomedical Research Involving Animals and many countries have developed regulations around the testing of animals. Review committees have to assess proposed animal testing and decide if it is necessary and passes certain standards. They look at ways to reduce or replace animal use and minimise suffering. This has led to many nations going offshore to conduct clinical trials on animals that don't pass local regulations.

issue:

WHAT IS YOUR OPINION ABOUT USING ANIMALS FOR LABORATORY TESTS? HOW DID YOU FORM YOUR OPINION?

clarify: PRIMATES, REGULATIONS, REVIEW COMMITTEES, ABOMINABLE

A university spokesperson yesterday said that 99 per cent of animals used at the university were rats and mice and that without laboratory testing on these rodents, the university would be unable to continue its research into cures for cancer.

However, according to an animal rights group spokesperson, some visiting scientists had been involved in overseas testing on primates in "abominable practices" and his group's website had disturbing video evidence of "horrific torture of innocent animals".

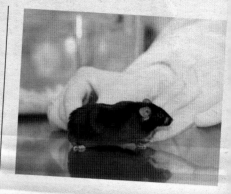

It is expected that there will be a strong police presence at the university on Friday to help keep protestors under control and minimise disruption of events.

...ALL CREATURES HAVE THE RIGHT TO LIFE

analyse:
DObES THE WRITER OF THIS ARTICLE PRESENT A BALANCED VIEW ABOUT THE PROS AND CONS OF VIVISECTION? WHY/WHY NOT?

PRO-ANIMALS: END THE SUFFERING – Join the Fight Against Testing on Animals!

news   home   about us   animals in research   press/photos   [   ]   search

> **general info**

> **species used in research**

> **news**

> **pain & distress**

> **ways to help**

> **videos**

join our online community

[first name]
[last name]
[your email]

join>>

ANTI-VIVISECTION RALLY THIS FRIDAY!

How would you feel if your family pet was put in a small cage, infected with nasty diseases and left to suffer a long, painful death? Every year between 50 and 100 million vertebrate animals are used in animal testing. These are not only rats and mice. Thousands of cats, dogs, rabbits and monkeys are tortured in experiments every year. In 2000 in the US, more than 25,000 cats were used in animal testing – around half of these were in experiments that had the potential to cause pain/distress.

Animal testing is terribly cruel and a lot of it is pointless. Results in animals are not directly transferable to humans. For example, while chocolate is edible for humans, it is toxic to dogs. Aspirin is a common household drug, but it is poisonous for cats.

According to the US Food and Drug Administration, 92 per cent of the drugs that were tested safe in animals failed during human trials. One anti-arthritis drug is an example. This drug was found to be safe after eight animal tests involving six different species. Yet it went on to kill more Americans than those who died in the Vietnam War. Testing on animals is not only cruel to animals, it is dangerous to humans.

clarify: ANTI-VIVISECTION RALLY, STATUS QUO, DESPICABLE, COMPUTER MODELLING

personal

WHAT RESPONSE
DOES THIS
INFORMATION
EVOKE IN YOU?

response

Many of the experiments performed on animals could be replaced with alternative methods, such as human tissue sampling and computer modelling. Unfortunately, scientists prefer to stick with the status quo and look likely to continue torturing and killing innocent animals for many years to come.

What makes this practice even more despicable is that there are many private competing organisations around the world conducting the same experiments on innocent animals. It is purely because of greed that these organisations do not share information and thousands of animals suffer needlessly in duplicated experiments.

We need to show our publicly elected government officials as well as the scientists who commit these atrocities that it is not okay to torture animals in the name of science. We will be holding an anti-vivisection rally on Friday at the science laboratory where government officials as well as scientists from around the country will be attending a conference. We'll create enough of a disturbance to make the national news, so people at home can hear our message about the unnecessary cruelty and torture that is taking place within our own country. **Join us in the fight!**

privacy policy | contact us |

question?

DID THE WRITER INFLUENCE/
CHANGE YOUR OPINION
ABOUT EXPERIMENTAL ANIMAL
TESTING IN LABORATORIES?
WHY/WHY NOT?

PRO-MEDICINE: SUPPORT ANIMAL TESTING!

Home   search   about us   news   research   projects

If your mother, father, sister or brother was suffering from a terrible terminal disease, wouldn't you do all you could to help them? Would you think that sacrificing the lives of a few laboratory rats was worthwhile if it led to advances in medicine that could save your loved one's life?

Animal experiments are essential to human survival. Virtually every medical achievement of the 20th century relied on the use of animals in some way. Millions of lives could have been lost if animal testing had not taken place.

Animal rights activists claim that animal testing can be replaced with computer modelling. If this were the case, it would have happened already. A report by the US National Academy of Sciences found that even very sophisticated computers cannot model the complex relationship between cells, molecules, tissues, organisms and the environment. A computer that could handle all of this would no doubt be cheaper and preferable to testing on animals and perhaps someday there will be such a machine, but at present the future health of the world's population relies on animal testing.

clarify: TERMINAL DISEASE, CELLS, MOLECULES, ORGANISMS, ETHICS COMMITTEE

emotional appeal:

HOW HAS THE AUTHOR USED EMOTIONAL APPEAL TO INFLUENCE YOUR OPINION?

PRO-MEDICINE: SUPPORT A   G!

Animal experiments are expensive, time-consuming and subject to regulations – the sole reason that animals are used is that they offer a more accurate result than any other method.

These experiments do not take place in some wild frontier land – they are heavily regulated. All experiments are governed by an ethics committee. In the US, for example, all experiments must be passed by the Institutional Animal Care and Use Committee. These ethics committees carefully weigh up the potential benefits of the experiments against the possibility of causing discomfort to animals. No animals will be harmed unless the experiment is necessary for the advancement of medicine.

A lot of protest material about animal testing uses images of domestic animals, yet these make up only a tiny percentage of the species used in animal testing. The majority of experiments use specially bred laboratory mice. These mice are the best model of inherited human disease, sharing 99 per cent of their genes with humans.

Animal experimentation is necessary. Our human survival depends on it. With luck, one day in the future it will no longer be necessary. But for now it is, and we have to put our trust in the very educated men and women who sit on the ethics committees around the world.

Join our organisation and say yes to human life over animal life!

privacy policy | contact us | site map

analyse:

ANALYSE THE INFORMATION ABOUT ANIMAL TESTING.

EVIDENTIAL INFORMATION?
(INFORMATION BASED ON FACT)

SUPPOSITIONAL INFORMATION?
(INFORMATION BASED ON POSSIBILITY)

BOYCOTT ANIMAL-

Voice your protest against this barbaric practice by hitting these companies where it hurts the most – their pockets! We have listed some of the cosmetic companies that test their products on animals. We urge you to stop supporting these companies immediately.

STOP THE CRUELTY:

A huge number of animals are needlessly suffering because of cosmetic testing. Have you ever seen a rabbit wearing makeup? Yet cosmetic companies perform all sorts of horrible tests on animals, despite the fact that they are not required to.

These companies are choosing to subject helpless animals to torture. There is a near total ban on this practice in the European Union and the UK. However, many countries, such as the US, continue the cruelty.

opinion:

WHAT IS YOUR OPINION ABOUT USING ANIMALS FOR LABORATORY TESTS? HOW DID YOU FORM YOUR OPINION?

Voice your PROTEST!

TESTED COSMETICS!

We have also included on our website a list of contact names and addresses for all of the companies. As well as boycotting their products, write to them and urge them to revise their animal-testing policies. These big companies need to get the message that what they are doing is wrong. You may only be one voice, but together we are powerful!

www.stopthecruelty.com

SAY NO to these companies!

They test their products on animals:

- Pella Cosmetics
- Rossani Beauty Products
- So Lovely Cosmetics
- Hendrich Haircare
- Nourishment Skincare

write in ... following
SAY NO ...

social action:

ARE BOYCOTTS OF PRODUCTS AN EFFECTIVE STRATEGY TO USE TO BRING ABOUT CHANGE IN A COMPANY'S PRACTICE? WHY/WHY NOT?

rhetorical question: FIND ANY?

clarify: FOREFRONT, RIGOROUSLY, PROPOSE

Animal Testing

To:	European Union
From:	Director, Pella Cosmetics
Subject:	Animal Testing

Received: 9.28am

To Whom It May Concern

I would like to voice my protest at the introduction of the European Union's ban on animal testing of cosmetics and the sale of cosmetics that have been tested on animals.

Our cosmetics company has a reputation for using the very best, safest ingredients. Our cosmetics are at the forefront of skin technology and are rigorously tested before use by humans to ensure that only the safest ingredients touch the skin of our customers. I am concerned that without this testing process we will be exposing our customers to unnecessary risk. Would you be happy to use makeup around your eyes if it had not been tested for the possibility of eye damage? Would you use shampoo on your child's head without knowing if it would cause a reaction with his/her skin?

Other cosmetics companies claim they do not test on animals. However, many of these companies use ingredients that have previously been trialled by companies such as ours. We don't want to use old technology in our product range. We know our customers want the latest advancements in skincare so we are continually developing and improving our ingredients to bring them the very best available products. It is essential that we properly test these products so we are not putting our customers at risk.

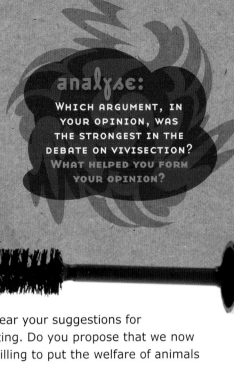

analyse:

WHICH ARGUMENT, IN YOUR OPINION, WAS THE STRONGEST IN THE DEBATE ON VIVISECTION? WHAT HELPED YOU FORM YOUR OPINION?

I would be interested to hear your suggestions for alternatives to animal testing. Do you propose that we now test on people? Are you willing to put the welfare of animals before that of your fellow human beings?

I urge you to reconsider the ban on animal testing and ensure that the cosmetic industry maintains the high safety standards that our customers rely on.

Yours truly,

Director
Pella Cosmetics
www.pellacosmetics.cc

summarise:

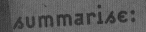

ARGUMENTS: ⊙ FOR VIVISECTION

⊙ AGAINST VIVISECTION

HOW WOULD YOU SUMMARISE THE KEY POINTS FOR EACH ARGUMENT?

Think about the Text

What connections can you make to the arguments and themes in *Viewpoint*?

HAVING AN OPINION

BELIEVING IN SOMETHING

EXPRESSING YOUR VIEW

text to Self

BEING OPEN-MINDED

TAKING A STANCE ON ISSUES

SEARCHING FOR THE TRUTH

BEING MANIPULATED

UNDERSTANDING BIAS

LISTENING TO ANOTHER POINT OF VIEW

text to Text/Media

Talk about other texts/media you have read, listened to or seen that have similar arguments/themes and compare the treatment of arguments/themes and the differing author styles.

text to World

Talk about situations in the world that might connect to elements in the text.

Planning a Persuasive Argument

Step one:

Decide on an issue/argument. Think about the viewpoint you will take.

REMORA FORUM: POST YOUR COMMENTS

FUR4EVA | POSTED: 10.01AM |

I am a supporter of the seal cull for ethical reasons. I consider hunted fur to be not only the environmentally friendly choice but also more humane than the alternatives.

Step two:

Research information to support your viewpoint. Look for:

factual material and viewpoints from magazines, journals and newspapers to provide supporting evidence

statements from experts or people familiar to the public

personal comments and views from fresh angles

particular examples to make the point

Think about ways you
can persuade people
to accept the main points
of your argument.
You can use:

endorsements from
experts and well-known
people or institutions

persuasive
language

statistics

emotional appeal
and language

A lot of anti-seal-cull protesters talk about
seals being skinned alive. However, a 2002
report by the *Canadian Veterinary Journal* found
that 98 per cent of the seals it examined had
been killed humanely. The Federal Department of
Fisheries and Oceans has also warned that looks
can be deceiving — seals have a swimming reflex
that is active even after death. This is similar to
the reflex seen in chickens.
It gives the impression of the animal being alive
and conscious, even though it is dead.

Think of an argument
that dismantles or rebuts
the contrary viewpoint.

Hunted fur has been used by
people for centuries. It is a
natural, eco-friendly product
obtained from animals that have
lived happily in their environment.
**I DON'T PLAN TO
STOP** WEARING IT
ANYTIME SOON.

Think of a conclusion
that supports the
initial statement.

Writing a Persuasive Argument

HAVE YOU...

- Clearly stated your topic and opinion by the end of the introductory paragraph?

- Used appropriate strategies of persuasion?

  for example:
  - › Appeal to emotions, such as fear, pity, love of tradition, desire for success, desire to conform, self-interest
  - › Thought-provoking descriptions and persuasive language, such as the use of words with strong positive/negative associations
  - › Analogies to help the reader identify with the text
  - › Personal endorsement

- Used factual and statistical information to support your argument?

- Used quotes from experts or familiar people?

- Used rhetorical questions?

- Rebutted the opposing point of view?

- Written a summarising conclusion to support your initial statement?

...don't forget to revisit your writing.

DO YOU NEED TO CHANGE, ADD OR DELETE ANYTHING TO IMPROVE YOUR ARGUMENT?